"Within four weeks I had written over 120,000 words. I had written a book! It waited patiently for me for 45 years. Without Tom, I never would have..."
Karen Stone, Smyra, Georgia

"Tom Bird is not only a teacher, mentor, but he is also a guide to listen to the heart of God."
Dorothy Wilt, co-author of Nursing the Spirit (American Nurses Association)

THE TOM BIRD METHOD™

You were born to. . .
Write

Complete Your Book in 30 Days or Less by Mastering the Inner Game of Writing

Tom Bird

The Tom Bird Method is a trademark of Tom Bird Seminars, Inc.

Requests for such permissions should be addressed to:
Sojourn, Inc.
P. O. Box 4306
Sedona, Arizona 86340
www.TomBird.com

Bird, Thomas J.
    You Were Born to. . . Write: Complete Your Book in 30 Days or Less by Mastering the Inner Game of Writing

Layout: J. L. Saloff
Photography: Mel Russell
Cover: Jane Perini
Fonts: Book Antiqua, Belwe, Tahoma, HelvCE

Paperback:
10 digit ISBN: 0-9789216-1-5
13 digit ISBN: 978-0-9789216-1-3

Hardcover:
10 digit ISBN: 0-9789216-0-7
13 digit ISBN: 978-0-9789216-0-6
Library of Congress Control Number: 2006907856

First Edition

Printed in the USA on acid free paper.

To Skyla;

You were born to _____
(You fill in the blank, Sweetheart, with what you
<u>choose</u> to do with your life and just know that your
Dad and Mom will do whatever they can to help
you live your Divine Purpose. That's just one of the
many reasons children have parents.)

We will always be there... Mom and Dad.

Contents

What You Will Need 5
   The Right Writing Utensils 7
   Paper 7
   Creative Writing 8
   Time 12
Setting Free Your Author Within 15
   Writing Principle #1 17
   Writing Principle #2 19
   Writing Principle #3 24
   Writing Principle #4 27
   Writing Principle #5 34
   Writing Principle #6 35
   Writing Principle #7 39
   Writing Principle #8 43
   Writing Principle #9 45
   Writing Principle #10 47
   Writing Principle #11 54
   Writing Principle #12 55
   Writing Principle #13 57
   Writing Principle #14 62
   Writing Principle #15 63
   Writing Principle #16 66
   Writing Principle #17 67

Moving On 69
Committing to Your Journey 71
   The Contract 71
     Your Written Commitment—Signed and Dated 72
Getting Started and YourLast Minute ChecklistBefore
Beginning 79
   A Few Last-Minute Insights to Keep in Mind that
   We Haven't Yet Covered 81
Your Second and Final Draft 85
   An Essential Point to Keep in Mind During this Draft 85
   Noting and Then Making Structural Changes 86
   Post-Writing Research 87
   The Colors of the Rainbow 87
   The Pianist in Us All 90
   Let Your Computer Go to Work for You 90
   One Final Read-Through 90
Crossing the Finish Line 93
   What I Have Discovered About Myself 93
   Your Next Book 94
   Publication and Sharing 95
About the Author 99

Introduction

YOU WERE BORN TO WRITE. YES, YOU READ THAT correctly — YOU — yes, YOU — were born to write. How else could you explain your obsessive draws to the craft: being a voracious reader; having ideas popping into your head at all hours of the day and night; never being able to shake your connection to this side of yourself, no matter how hard you tried or how unqualified or untalented you felt at times?

In recorded history, it was Aristotle who first recognized and then commented upon the far-reaching significance of this art we call writing. In fact, he believed that for a person to live a full life, he or she had to not only build a home and raise a child but write a book as well.

This same acknowledgment of the importance of writing is consciously alive in more of us today than ever before. In fact, a survey recently quoted in The New York Times claimed that 81% of Americans admitted to believing they had a book inside of them.

I know God will not give me anything I can't handle.
I just wish that He didn't trust me so much.

Mother Teresa

After appearing before over 50,000 aspiring writers through over 3,000 lectures on over 100 college and university campuses over the last 23 years, I would have to agree with the results of that survey, even though I feel the results were only off by a mere 19%. Yes, I do feel that everyone at one time or another in their lives—some for sixty years and some for six minutes after a six-pack of beer—come in contact with who I refer to as their "author within," who more than anything else wants them to experiencee the joy, growth, and overall significance that comes with the writing of a book.

And. yes, after all of my work with aspiring writers, I believe that each one of us has at least one book inside calling to be born, if not for publication, then for ourselves as a quick and direct route to self-revelation and self-love. As a result, I feel that everyone should write. In fact, I firmly feel that if everyone every day took a little time to better connect with whatever ultimate source they believed to be out there through writing, and squeezed in a nap every afternoon, more would be done to eradicate the envy, jealousy, and hatred that plagues the world than anyone thought imaginable.

My role in this book is to serve as your literary mid-wife. As a result, it will be my job to offer you all of the direction, assistance, and encouragement you deserve to birth that book or books that have been calling out to you. I can guarantee that if you follow my instructions to the letter, whatever book or books that are presently inside you will be released in their entirety as quickly, effectively, and successfully as possible. However; I cannot promise the process will be pain-free. I can promise you though that any pain can be severely minimized if you limit your resistance to this process. For, in essence, pain is nothing more than resistance to growth. Halt the resistance and the pain falls by the wayside. So it is up to you whether to experience pain or how much pain you choose to undergo. The key to how much pain you may choose to feel lies in your resistence to replacing the habits that have held you back as a writer with actions, thoughts, and philosophies that will enable you to return to the natural, expressive, God-connected state in which we were all born.

We do not write in order to be understood;
we write to understand.

C. Day Lewis
The Poetic Image

This book and the book or books you will write will change your life. This book will do so, especially in the beginning, by identifying, challenging, and then removing the limiting beliefs that have kept you from the birthing all of who you are. It will then offer you the fail-proof, step-by-step system, which I have been sharing for nearly a quarter of a centruy, to release your book, safely, naturally, and comfortably, and pain-free if you would like, in as little as a few days to just over a month. It will then share with you a series of steps you can take to polish your manuscript. Lastly, it will offer you an overview of all you have learned through your work with it as well as a severely shortened methodology for the writing of any further works.

Do not fear death so much, but rather the inadequate life.

Bertoit Brecht

I first developed this system for myself, then an aspiring writer, after all of the orthodox methods I studied and applied had failed miserably. I did so by first asking for divine guidance in this area and then receiving it. The result of the method I was led to develop astounded even me. Not only did I become the published author my soul cried out for me to be, but my outlook on myself, my life, and my divine purpose was significantly sharpened as well. I would never be the same person I was after employing the following system. I was forever and for better changed. Thank God. The same will happen for you as well.

Tom Bird

What You Will Need

Y OU HAVE PROBABLY BEEN IN THE STATE BEFORE. YOU KNOW, the one where words poured out of you and flowed onto the paper at a rate you almost could not keep up with. That state, which I will be introducing you to, is the foundation for the transition that I have spoken of as well as for the completion of your book or books using this system. Yes, writing fast is not only good but necessary. For the faster you write the more time you are devoting to how you feel and the less you are putting aside for thinking. Since writing, especially during the essentially expressive first draft, is a heart art, based around sharing your most in-depth feelings, as opposed to one based around thinking and the intellect, it is essential that it be done fast.

This all-fulfilling journey you are about to embark upon will not take long, but you will need the following to successfully complete it.

Success Story by Bonnie Sanchez

From: Bonnie Sanchez, Seattle, Washington
To: Tom Bird

This book is a must read for everyone. Even if you think you have no interest in writing. I promise you, before you finish this book, you will have a desire to write. You won't be able to stop yourself. You'll be scribbling on the back of your gas receipt at a stoplight. When you follow Tom's methods, your creative energy just flows. Characters will come to you and just start talking. You grab the nearest piece of paper and writing utensil you can find and just let it flow. I know there are a lot of people struggling to fulfill their dream of writing a book and getting it published. I know a lot of people think it takes years. It doesn't have to. When you follow Tom's methods, you will understand why it doesn't have to take that long. Tom has a gift. And he's willing to share it with the rest of us. Take advantage of his kindness. He's not only an amazing writer and teacher, but his spiritual insights are very enlightening as well. I hooked up with Tom to become a writer, but I've become so much more. Thank you, Tom!

The Right Writing Utensils

Don't worry or flip out. I'm not saying that you shouldn't, or we won't, at some point focus on revising, correcting, or editing what you have written. In fact, we will go into that in great detail later. All I am saying is that when you are initially composing, it is best to go with the speed of the flow and not inhibit it by trying to revise, review, or correct it at the same time you are writing it. That's all.

To best maintain the speed by which it will come pouring out of you, you will need the right writing utensil. What that translates to is a pen that transfers a lot of ink to the ball, so as to better lubricate the flow of it along the fibers of your paper.

So I would very strongly suggest a bit of time set aside to testdrive a few pens at your local office supply store. Pick the one or ones that flow the best and feel the most comfortable in your hand. For a writer, choosing the right pen is as important as the choice of the right shoes for a runner.

Paper

Yes, you're initially going to do your writing on paper–large, lineless sheets of paper to be exact. What I recommend are 14x17 drawing pads: two of them, for the initial writing of your book.

I realize that writing on paper may be a stretch for you. For one, you may be keyboard-dependent and as a result feel that you do your best writing with you fingers blazing across the keys. To that notion I respond by saying that you have not yet done your best writing. If you had, you wouldn't be in need of this book. Secondly, you won't feel the peace you deserve to experience as a writer until you have effectively and completely released whatever is dying to be released from you. So if you have been writing but have not yet experienced that feeling of peace and completion that all successful writers enjoy, you have not yet done your best writing, and your addictive tie to your keyboard is one major reason why.

You see, your use of the keyboard ties you to your thinking mind and completely gets in the way of your expressive mind during the writing process, and, as a result, really mucks up things. So we want to stay as far away as possible from any association with a keyboard during the conversionary process you will be going through.

Secondly, you may not feel comfortable writing in longhand because your writing is illegible. Don't worry. It is only illegible at the present time. Of course, there are many factors that contribute to that, all of which will be removed when you begin employing this process. As a result, your handwriting, reflecting your appreciation for your newfound state of being, will change as well and become legible, because it seeks to be read and you will seek to share it.

Get the paper along with the right writing utensils so we can move on. In fact, don't read the next section until you come home with your drawing pads and pen.

Creative Writing

I can guarantee you that every bit of writing that has ever positively influenced your life, mood, or day was written by an author in an "Author Within" (AW) connected state. So essential is this state that many an author has agonized needlessly, for sometimes as long as decades, because they didn't know how to get into this state. Mostly this is because they had been erroneously informed that the inspiration they sought was only accessible through an outside influence referred to as the Muse, who chooses, most haphazardly of course, who and when to visit.

Nothing could be further from the truth. The artistic expression we all seek, which lifts each one of us to greater heights and finally sets us free, is only accessible by turning inward. Of course, even though how one is capable of doing this has been documented scientifically and psychologically for decades, as a culture we have not yet left behind our former limited beliefs to make room for the solutions that await us. More on that later.

We are traditionally rather proud of ourselves for having slipped creative work in there in between the domestic chores and obligations. I'm not sure we deserve such big A-pluses for that.

Toni Morrison

What getting into this essential state all boils down to is following what I refer to as the Three Rs of Writing, which refer to:

1. Reserving Time To Write (the best time of which is after a nap or a good night's sleep);

2. Removing Distractions (turn off the phone and inform those who you are closest to and/or live with when you will be writing so they won't bother you);

3. Relaxing (when the first two Rs are followed, you will move directly into an "Author Within" connected state, when the relaxing of your mind clears the way for the opening of your heart or Creative Connected Mind-CCM-through which your AW speaks).

God tells me how He wants this music played—
and you get in His way.

Arturo Toscanini

Each of the above needs to be strictly adhered to each time you sit down to write or each time you review your writing. This is where the discipline of writing comes so strongly into play. If you take the time to follow the Three Rs of Writing each time you write or review your work, everything will go great. If you don't, your mind will get in the way and it won't. It's as simple as that.

> "I feel excited about waking up in the morning, and I awake earlier to accomplish my goals. I can only imagine what I can accomplish if I follow through on my commitment to myself and keep it up.
> Vicki, student, New Mexico

Admittedly, the first two Rs are pretty easy to deal with. Set aside time to write after a nap or an evening of sleep, unplug the phone during writing times and speak to your friends and family, asking them to leave you alone during those times.

It's the third R, relaxing, that most people have a difficult time with. In most cases it is because they either don't know how to relax or they try too hard to do so. As a result, many of them end up studying meditation or taking medication to do so, neither of which is necessary.

Relaxing translates to quieting the mind by putting it to sleep. To do so, simply follow these steps:

1. Sit up straight with your feet flat on the floor and your arms and legs uncrossed;

2. Close your eyes;

3. Smile broadly for a minute or so to lighten and brighten your mood (it's nearly impossible to relax if you're not calm, and it's not possible to be calm unless you're happy);

4. Breath deeply through your nose and exhale even more deeply through your mouth (do this for ten consecutive breaths)

Once you are relaxed, your mind is now calm and the route to your AW, through which all inspiration comes, is open. Then all you have to do is toss a catalyst its way to offer it a focus and/or direction (a theme or whatever — more on this later too) and it will take off writing.

Keep away from the people who try to belittle your ambitions. Small people always do that, but the really great make you feel that you, too, can become great.

Mark Twain

I know that for some of you the above may appear easy, but I also realize that there are many of you who are what my close friend and student Sharon Lamm-Hartman, the author of a book on the subject, would refer to as "recovering intellectuals." For you, because of an extensive education in a non-creative field or as the result of an abuse suffered, your mind, which in your case may be responsible for leading you and/or protecting you, may be less willing to step aside. If that is the case, I don't suggest that you throw yourself into a deep study of meditation or begin to medicate. No, what I simply suggest is that you purchase a copy of a subliminal/self hypnosis tape that I have been recommending for the last twenty-five years entitled Creative Writing by Potentials Unlimited, which has been in business providing these sorts of options for decades. Through utilizing the subliminal side of the tape, you will, without any extensive preparation, be able to plug into your AW state whenever and wherever you want. Even though the tape is available for ordering through bookstores, I recommend going to their website, potentialsunlimited.com, and purchase it for download.

Time

As mentioned above, you will have to start setting aside time to write on a consistent basis. It is essential that you utilize the methods included in this book on a consistent basis, to best replace what has not been working for you with what I guarantee will lead you to the success you deserve.

What does "consistent" equate to? Initially, it equates to six days a week.

How much time is necessary each day? Optimally, you want to be writing a consistent two hours, six days a week, by the time you reach the section on the writing of your book. However, if you have to start out more slowly to best work writing into your schedule, do so. Just make sure that you are up to that two hours a day by the end of the next section, which will be essential to your success.

I know it may be difficult to get yourself to consistently sit down and write. I promise all of that will change though. All you have to do is keep disciplining yourself for the first few days to sit down and follow the Three Rs of Writing. By then, the positive effects of your efforts begin to take hold. Once that transpires, you will become positively addicted to the Divine connection you reach through your writing.

Grasshopper, look beyond the game, as you look beneath the surface of the pool to see its depths.

Master Po
Kung Fu

Setting Free Your Author Within

A NY LACK OF SUCCESS YOU MAY HAVE EXPERIENCED UP TO this point with writing has nothing to do with you. In fact, there is nothing wrong with you as a writer, with the exception of the fact that you did what you were told and believed what was shared with you.

"Our loss begins in school, when the process of writing is taught to us in fragments: mechanics, grammar, and vocabulary," says Gabriele Lusser Rico, author of *Writing the Natural Way* (Tarcher). "Writing becomes fearful and loathsome, a workbook activity. Students write as little as possible, and once out of school, they tend to avoid the entire process whenever possible. As a result, few people turn to writing as a natural source of pleasure and gratification."

You see, no matter how caring whatever educational system you were exposed to may have been and no matter how hardworking your teachers, what you were taught about how to write and what was possible for you as a writer was all off-base. The reason for this error was that the breakthroughs that needed to happen to better understand the art form did not transpire until a few decades ago. What you had been taught had been around for potentially hundreds of years by that time, and it takes decades for the correct information to be integrated into our school systems. And the ineffective methodology you were exposed to about writing is just now, ever so slowly, starting to be replaced. So you can see this book as a fast forwarding to replace what you were taught with what you, as a writer, would have, instead, substantially benefited from.

"A lot of people in English departments should never be trusted to run a program," states author Wallace Stegner. "Their training is all in the other direction, all analytical, all critical. It's all reader's training, not a writer's training, so they have no notion of how to approach the opportunity."

Like inserting car keys into the right ignition and finally being able to turn over the engine, once you have employed the following changes you can immediately expect massive gains, as you return to the natural, expressive ability we are all born with.

Education made us what we are.

Claude-Adrien Helvetius

Each of the following seventeen principles of writing have been designed to counteract each one of the specific beliefs that in one way or another have held back your development. Approach each one of the following statements in the same manner, utilizing your scheduled writing time to do so six days a week:

1. Use either your Creative Writing CD or follow the Three Rs of Writing to get yourself in an AW connected state;

2. Then position yourself in front of a mirror, look yourself straight in the eye, and repeat, one at a time, each writing principle to yourself;

3. As you do so, write down any responses you may have to the principle on one of the large drawing pads positioned at your side;

4. Continue to repeat each statement, even if some take several sessions each, until you can look yourself in the eye in the mirror, repeat the statement, and feel absolutely nothing, either positive or negative–then and only then will the effects of each statement have been cleansed from your perspective.

Writing Principle #1

The Past Does Not Determine the Future

A lot of what I refer to as "writing refugees" (WRs) attend my classes, seminars, workshops, and retreats.

By my definition, WRs are persons who have previously, at one level or another, studied writing without having experienced the success to which they aspired.

In most cases, over the years, these persons have utilized a variety of excuses to justify their lack of success: not having enough time, talent, education; not having anything of substance anyone, including themselves, would want to read. Rarely have those I have been exposed to chosen to put the blame for their lack of success on anything or anyone outside their own selves, which was completely opposite of the truth. For the reason they had not succeeded up to this point had nothing to do with themselves, but instead with what they had been taught.

Creative minds always have been known to survive any kind of bad training.

Anna Freud

A PhD clinical psychologist attended one of my classes several years ago in Virginia. I got a chance to sit down and speak with her for a few minutes before our first class together, and I was amazed at all the effort she had put into her writing up to that point without experiencing the success she desired.

She had spent years attempting to write. She had designated a room in her home as her "writing space." She had read dozens of books on the craft and still nothing was happening for her.

After just one weekend of proper instruction, she was on her way to being the published author she had felt drawn to be for so long. Having gotten better in touch with her AW in regard to what it was that she was being led to write, she took her now crystal-clear idea out to literary agents, the commissioned-based, necessary liaisons between especially new authors and book publishers. In no time at all, over dozens of agents had expressed interest in the representation of her book, which wasn't even written. After aligning herself with the agent who was the best match, her representative sold her book in about three weeks.

This same person has continued with her writing and has since published several more books. If she, like so many thousands of others in her situation, had not believed in the fact that The Past Does Not Determine the Future, she would have never been open to doing something different than she had been doing up to that point. As a result, she would never have come to my classes, learned a different route, and gone on to the success she has since enjoyed.

Writing Principle #2

We Alone Are Responsible for
Creating Our Own Successes

I came to the principles that I share in this book through Divine intervention. That's right; tired of failing miserably as an aspiring writer, I had finally gotten desperate enough to seek God's assistance. So desperate was I that I promised to share with others whatever He/She presented so that those others wouldn't have to suffer as badly as I was at that moment. In my opinion, there's nothing worse than having a dream stuck inside of you without a route for releasing it.

Two nights after I made my request, the reply I was seeking came in the form of a vision, waking me up in the middle of the night. In the vision I saw exactly how I needed to approach both the writing of books and publishing, now referred to as *The Tom Bird Method*™. Once put into play, the rights to my first book were sold about six weeks later to Harper & Row, and I received an advance for it equivalent to three times the salary I was earning as The Assistant Director of Publicity with the big league's Pittsburgh Pirates.

After signing a contract with my publisher, I began work on my book. Using the principles I was shown, I completed the writing of the 110,000-word manuscript in less than three months, all of which was done while working seven days a week, and an average of sixteen hours a day, for the Pirates. Shortly after completing the book, I resigned from my position with Pittsburgh and began offering classes at local colleges and universities as a way of sharing my method.

You have to leave the city of your comfort and go into the wilderness of your intuition. What you'll discover will be wonderful. What you'll discover will be yourself.

Alan Alda

After two years of teaching I figured I had fulfilled whatever promise I had made, so I decided to revisit whether I wanted to continue teaching or not. In doing so, the first question I asked myself was whether I still enjoyed the teaching, and my reply was "Yes." Then I asked myself if there was anything I would change about the teaching if I could. At that moment, my mind was flooded with a series of images of students who had attended my courses, who weren't in any way ready for what I had to offer. As a result they had fought accepting my guidance.

So I decided to continue teaching, but I asked God that I not be sent any more "green apples." Since that time, I can honestly say that I have not had students who registered for my classes who were not ready to take the bull by the horns and bring their success to them.

The world is packed full of people who are just not ready. You know the ones I mean–those who are continually making excuses why they are not doing this or that which they supposedly want to do, and who continually, in one way or another, sabotage their own efforts. We've all been there. Maybe you were there before you picked this book. Maybe the reason you did pick up this book was because you were ready to finally take responsibility for you own success.

I know that I wasn't ready to accept that responsibility until I finally had the conversation with God, which I mentioned above. But by then I was really ready.

It is said that no one makes a major change in his or her life until the pain gets so great that he or she has to, and I was sure in a lot of pain by that point. Nothing in my life was working. I guess you could say that the desperation I was experiencing was the forefather of my readiness. Based upon my own experiences and those of my students, I have come to see the true importance and necessity of desperation. "Desperation," as I like to say, "is the forefather of faith."

He must forget the things he does not wish to remember and remember only the things he wishes to retain.

Baird T. Spalding
Life and Teaching of the Masters of the Far East

Take a moment to ponder the situation and feelings you were experiencing before you picked up this book. What led you to read it? The encouragement or complaining of those closest to you? Other signs that may have popped up as well? Your own pain and dissatisfaction with at least this area of your life? What?

Whatever it is that got you to this point has changed you. You are finally ready to create your own success. You are no longer allowing the past to determine your future.

The methods shared in this book and another of my works, *You Were Born to Be... Published*, will lead you to the success you desire. Not only can I attest to this through my own success but also through that of tens of thousands of my students who have gone on to write books and to publish. There is no longer anything standing in your way, and that which was halting your progress, a certain part of you, has been set off to the side of the road.

Even the publishing industry is not standing in your way. As I show in my book on publishing, it doesn't matter to those in the industry whether you have a degree or not, or what your age or color or socio-economic background is. If you have a passion for something that you want to communicate in writing and are both familiar with and employ the right etiquette, you will find that a strong percentage of them are more than happy to consider either publishing or representing your work to publishers.

Myra was a student of mine who attended one of my weekend classes in Knoxville. For the longest time, Myra, who was a very driven writer, had been faithfully attending a monthly writer's group in her local area, and had gone absolutely nowhere with getting her book written and/or published.

I set Myra straight on the information that had been shared with her and what she needed to do to make the dream of writing her book a reality. So excited was she with what I had to offer her that she couldn't wait to share it with the fellow members of her writing group. Much to her surprise though, her offering of the information I had shared with her was met with a staunch rejection she never expected.

Lesson: Misery does love company. Those in Myra's writer's group had always used this excuse or that one to justify their lack of success with their writing. Never once had they ever looked at themselves as the potential cause of that failure and, as a result, when Myra offered them the solutions that they were supposedly opened to, they instead rejected everything she had to share.

Pain is inevidable, suffering is optional.

M. Kathleen Casey

Myra left the group shortly afterward. She simply was no longer willing to be a part of a group that would not take responsibility for their own success or, in this case, was so communally frightened of succeeding that they took turns sabotaging each other's efforts.

When Myra left the group, she took back control of her life, put into play what she had learned in my class, and finished her first book less than a month later. **We alone are responsible for creating our own successes.**

So much about life is just about showing up. Many people show up physically for work or for life, but does every part of them show up? No. In most cases, their body may be there, but their heart, desire, and mind are not. Because so few people do so, all you have to do to succeed in this life is to show up–all of you–your heart, your soul, your attention, your desire–YOU!

By reading this book and employing the methods in it, you are taking responsibility for creating your own success by showing up and, as a result, you can expect your results to change dramatically in the near future.

Writing Principle #3

Writing Can Be Fast, Easy, and Fun

Remember, we alone are responsible for creating our own successes. If you're incorrectly going about any task, whether it is writing or something else, it will always be difficult or downright unsuccessful if you are approaching it incorrectly. That's right, you've been doing things wrong. Is that your fault? No. You were just taught to go about it wrongly. How could that be the case? Billions are spent on our educations and the training of our teachers and professors each year. Do I mean to say that the money devoted to writing has been squandered on incorrect philosophies and approaches? Yes.

Just think about it for a minute. If you are enrolled in a college class on nursing let's say, there's an excellent chance that the professor teaching the course is a proven, certified nurse. The same goes for other areas such as law, other medical fields, accounting, psychology, education, business, and any of the sciences.

However, what do you get when you take a college course on writing? Is the person a proven author, a successful writer? Probably not. So basically what that means is that they are not really qualified to teach you something that they have not yet accomplished, nor are they capable of distinguishing between what is right and wrong. And who designed the writing curriculum? You guessed it—people just as unqualified to be teaching writers as they were.

And what do you receive from these persons? In depth instruction on how to follow in their exact footsteps, which will lead you to where as a writer? To the same lack of success that they themselves experienced. Is it any wonder then that you are where you are as a writer? Is it any wonder that writing has been just so darn hard and painful for you? Why again would that be the case? Because you simply did as you were told and followed in the footsteps of those who taught you everything you know about the craft. And, again, those persons were? Failed writers.

Most books on writing are filled with bullshit. Fiction writers, present company included, don't even understand very much about what they do—not why it works when it's good, not why it doesn't when it's bad.

Stephen King
On Writing: A Memoir of the Craft

However it's not their fault that they shared with you what they did. They were doing the best they could; plus they didn't know better. You see, as I mentioned in the Introduction, because of a lack of understanding associated with the craft of writing, which has been around for centuries, how to properly approach it remained basically a mystery until some necessary breakthroughs transpired in the late sixties. Even though the results of those breakthroughs have been around for almost four decades, they have been slow to be integrated into our educational system because it is so large and bureaucratic, and thus slow to change.

Putting all of that aside, let's approach this subject from a more positive perspective. I am assuming that there were times when your writing just seemed to flow out of you. Were there not? Of course there were, which is one of the many reasons you have stayed with your desire to write for so long. You felt the flow, you know it exists, and it feels so darn good. You just don't know how to get to it.

He writes as fast as they can read, and he does not write himself down.

William Hazlitt

My old buddy Jack who now lives in Orlando has found his niche as a golfer, a game he has continually encouraged me to take up. Kidding, I tell my old friend that I am not old enough to take it up yet, because I am still more than capable of participating in much more physical activities.

Jack always counters by saying something to the effect that, "If I could get you out on the course and just once, even it if was by accident, you hit the ball just right and heard that magical 'ping,' you'd be hooked for life." I know that to be the case, of course, which is really why I haven't taken up the game. I consider myself too busy with other things to become "hooked for life."

I know this situation well, as do you. For I have seen tens of thousands of people enter into my classes, who were hooked to their writing for life. It is those persons who have heard, experienced, and felt the "ping" of writing, which is exactly what has kept them coming back to it for so long.

Now all you have to do is to learn how to hear that "ping" every time you approach your writing. Then and only then, not only will you be writing well, but enjoying it and succeeding at too, which is the entire purpose behind not only the next few principles, but this entire book as well.

Writing Principle #4

All of the Inspiration
We Will Ever Need Is Already Inside of Us

I apologize for any shock or disappointment that the following statements may cause, but there is no Easter Bunny (Santa Claus I'm still not to sure about) and there is no such thing as the Muse, the mystical, magical being and/or essence that supposedly visits artists from the outside whenever it wants, and if it ever wants.

For centuries the Muse has served as both a sense of frustration and madness amongst artists and a cause for exhilaration. When the Muse visited, all went well: masterpieces were painted on the ceilings of famous chapels; classic novels were written, and majestic sculptures magically evolved. When the Muse was absent, drunkenness, dereliction, depression, madness, and suicide often transpired, as supposedly powerless but passionate artists lamented upon what it was that they had to do, where they had to be, or what they had to say to once again attract the Muse back into their lives.

With this belief so firmly rooted in place with so many classic writers, from Kerouac to Hemingway to Wolfe, is it any wonder that so much dereliction became associated with such a blessed craft, the brilliance of which, in reality, is available to every person, no matter what his or her station in life?

So extensively absurd has our culture's belief been in this area that a movie was actually produced on the topic, featuring award-winning actress Sharon Stone, entitled The Muse. In the movie, all who visited Stone, who was the Muse, received magical, creative, expressive powers, much like what the artists of the past believed. When they were out of her favor though, all they had been given disappeared and they slumped greatly, not only as artists but personally as well.

Of course, none of this is true, unless, of course, you choose to believe it and choose to create that as you own reality, or decide to employ it as your excuse to keep you from doing what it is that your heart calls you to do.

The truth is that access to the inspiration we all seek is inside each one of us, which is why you have never been able to outrun it no matter how hard you tried. It was always right there, all the time, inside of you. It's impossible to outrun yourself, so, it is impossible to outrun the inspiration trying to stream out of you.

All of Jesus' healings were on the basis of
removing the mental cause.

Baird T. Spalding
Life and Teaching of the Masters of the Far East

The base of this inspiration is housed in the Creative Connected Mind (CCM), whose primary purpose is to express your Divine purpose or message in an unconditional, passionate way.

If this is such a natural state, what then has kept your writing from flowing freely at all times? Once again, that's all tied to the improper education of your LCM, or Logical Critical Mind–your other, more logic-based side.

You see, there couldn't be two more complete opposites than your LCM and CCM. The LCM's primary purpose is to avoid pain. Your CCM's primary purpose is to express the results of your heartfelt connection with the Divine.

The LCM communicates through thinking, analyzing, and criticizing while the CCM utilizes feelings.

The LCM is conditional. It always comes from one perspective and one perspective only: will whatever it is that you are about to partake in cause you pain? If so, it will avoid it at all costs.

The CCM is unconditional by nature. It's always honest and heartfelt. It feels, it expresses, it doesn't worry about repercussions, and why should it since it never comes from a place of malice?

The LCM has very limited capabilities. In fact, when you were born, your LCM was like a blank hard drive. It knew absolutely nothing. And everything it learned from that point forward came from conditioning: rote and repetition associated with your five senses.

On the other hand, your CCM has unlimited capabilities because it draws from the much higher perspective of a direct connection with your Source. You've probably already experienced on a firsthand basis when gems of brilliance came flowing through your writing, and you knew not from where they came. Well now you know where they originated–from your CCM's direct connection with the Source.

Within the LCM is housed your short-term memory, whose lone connection to the world is limited to only that which enters into it consciously through the five senses.

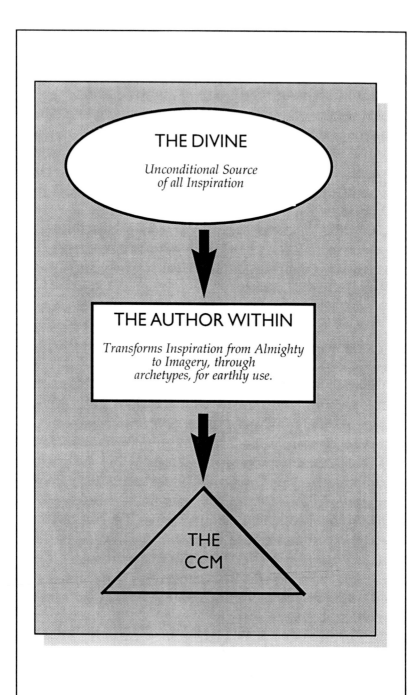

Once received, this skeletal interpretation is housed for a very short period of time before being released, which is why, while in your LCM, you may not have been able to account for exactly what you were doing only a few hours before.

Conversely, just like the Source, the CCM draws from a much deeper connection to life than the five senses and has storage capabilities far greater than the LCM, which is why, while in a CCM state, you are able to recall, with great richness and feeling, incidents that transpired years, if not decades, before.

The CCM draws from, or at times expresses through, its long-term memory to access the depth, color, feeling, analogy, and most of all the universality needed to touch hearts, including your own.

The LCM sleeps while the CCM doesn't.

Have you ever awakened in the middle of the night and needed to write? Have you ever been driving along in your car and all of a sudden, out of nowhere, your mind was overwhelmed by an inspiration you had to capture on paper? How about when you are relaxing on vacation and this same inspiration visits you? What do all of these occurrences have in common? In each and every case your LCM had been asleep or unguarded, allowing your connection with your CCM to finally come streaming through.

Why does a state such as this one have to exist before you are able to connect with this obviously powerful, all-seeing source, the CCM?

The answer to that question is simple but far reaching.

When you were born, as exhibited by your free flowing, expressive, heartfelt, unconditional, spontaneous living patterns at the time, being directly connected to your Source through your CCM was natural, until being so open and expressive led to pain. This transition in the acceptance of the true-you probably happened around the time when you were two. Until then, you had probably been pretty well unconditionally accepted. But by the time you were two, you had learned to speak and speak you did, maybe too often, too loudly, too openly, and too honestly.

Creative activity could be described as
a type of learning process where the teacher and the
pupil are located in the same individual.

Arthur Koestler

As Don McLean captured in his song "Vincent," about Vincent Van Gogh, "the world was never meant for someone as beautiful as you."

No, the world that your parents, your family, your town or city had been overwhelmed by, and that they were sharing with you, was the result of an unnatural LCM world, which did not appear to be meant for someone as beautiful as you. Yet, at the same time, this same lost, confused, and overwhelmed world desperately needs persons such as you. In fact, anyone who had ever changed the world in any positive way had been in a spirit-connected CCM state when they had done so.

However, those who have most directly influenced your life were just afraid. They didn't want you to be subjected to the same pain they been exposed to. At other times, their fears took the form of a destroy-at-all-costs envy.

All were effective teachers though. As a result, your LCM began to associate the deep, heartfelt connection you

The Characteristics of Your LCM Versus Your CCM

Your LCM:

Purpose:
Avoid Pain

Thinks, Evaluates,
Criticizes

Conditional

Limited Capabilities

Short-Term Memory

Sleeps

Falsely Dominant

Your CCM:

Purpose:
Expression

Feels

Unconditional

Unlimited Capabilities

Long-Term Memory

Never Sleeps

Innately Dominant

feel with your writing with the same part of you that was not accepted as a child. Since then, your LCM has done everything possible to keep you from associating with this Source-led connection, which is why it has fought to keep you from writing. This is also why it may have ruthlessly judged/criticized whatever it was that you did write. It just didn't want you to be hurt through the sharing of your writing with anyone else. That's all. So in this way, your LCM has been a very good friend. However, all of the actions it has taken in regard to your writing have been taken while acting under the influence of an inappropriate education.

To reverse all that it has learned, and to get it on our side–as it has been in so many other successful endeavors in your life–all we have to do is retrain it, which is one of the major focuses of this book.

We are all dancing on a volcano

Comte De Salvandy

Writing Principle #5

We Can Access a Connection to
Our Unlimited Expression at Any Time

If you have been following the instructions for the above exercises, you already know this to be true. And how have you accessed this inspiration, wrongly referred to as the Muse? Simple. Through the 3Rs of Writing, which you have hopefully been employing through your participation in the exercises above. How can one access their Author Within? Through the Three Rs of Writing. How can a person continue to deepen and strengthen this most exciting of all connections? By continuing to use the Three Rs on a regular basis, until connecting with and living through this connection becomes as natural and routine as breathing, just as it was meant to be.

> *Tom knows where the words come from and is a master at teaching your author within to allow them to effortlessly flow onto the paper. Thanks, Tom.*
> *George Wallach, author of Harvest of Illusion (HighSight Publishing)*

The failure of outer things to satisfy leads
the soul to seek the power within.

Baird T. Spalding
Life and Teaching of the Masters of the Far East

Writing Principle #6

You Have a Very Special Message to Share Through Your Writing

My exposure to so many persons of different backgrounds, ages, beliefs, and life experiences for so long has made it very clear to me that every person has a very special message to share through whatever it is that he or she feels drawn to write.

Success Story by Diana Theordores

From: Diana Theordores, U. K.
To: Tom Bird

Purely by chance I saw Tom's workshop advertised in the University of New Mexico special courses literature and enrolled. When this young man with hair flowing down past his shoulders walked into the seminar room, I have to admit I sneered mentally. What does he think he's going to teach ME about writing? By the end of the session, I was the first person to sign up to work with Tom on his intensive course, with one-on-one mentoring. What he had to say about writing as a physical act made sense. What he had to say about needing physical stamina and conditioning in order to maintain flow made sense. What he had to say about writing as releasing rather than constructing made sense. What he had to say about discipline made sense. And his optimistic attitude towards time made sense: why not get as much done in as short a time as possible? What was a revelation for me was that all the items on my wish list (physical discipline, release, sustained focus, writing from the heart, finished product) were integrated here in one method of working and living.

I wrote 194,000 words on large poster boards in five weeks, and the experience was exhilarating and provocative.

It really doesn't matter what you write or what form your writing takes. As long as it springs forth from your AW, it will not only be good but what the Source within you was attempting to express through you. Even if the book that came streaming through you ended up being a light, little romance, it could still be considered a work of significance if it made people smile, laugh, cry, or feel, and, in doing so, touched their hearts. For how many run-ins that you experience each day actually touch you deeply? Again, it is not the form your writing takes that determines the significance of what you wrote as much as how it affected, and if it did affect, the lives, minds, and–mostly–the hearts of those who came in contact with it.

Talent alone cannot make a writer.
There must be a man behind the book.

Ralph Waldo Emerson

The only decision we need to make in this regard is this: "Do we open ourselves up to that unique, unconditional love and acceptance offered to us by our Creator and allow that very special message to be shared with everyone we come in contact with, including our own selves, or do we continue to avoid that most unique of all gifts and continue to live in the pain and despair of the masses, avoiding the call to be the leader we were born to be?"

By choosing to read and write your way through this book, I believe you have already made that decision. Congratulations on the choice you have made.

Our deepest fear is not that we are inadequate.
Our deepest fear is that we are
Powerful beyond measure.
It is our Light, not our
Darkness, that most frightens us.
We ask ourselves, Who am I to be brilliant,
Gorgeous, talented, fabulous?
Actually, who are you not to be?
You are a child of God.
Your playing small does not serve the World.
There is nothing enlightening about
Shrinking so that other people
Won't feel unsure around you.
We were born to make manifest the
Glory of God that is within us.
It is not just in some of us; it is in everyone.
As we let our own Light shine,
We unconsciously give other people
Permission to do the same.
As we are liberated from our own fear,
Our presence automatically
Liberates others.

Nelson Mandela*

*As quoted by Marianne Williamson in her book Reflections on the
Principles of a Course in Miracles, Harper Collins, ©1992

Writing Principle #7

Fast Writing Is Always the Best Writing

As I mentioned earlier, I can guarantee you that every bit of writing that has ever positively influenced your life, mood, or day was written by someone who wrote it while in an "Author Within" connected state. I can also guarantee you that while this person was in this state that they were writing fast. Yes, fast. Writing fast is essential because the faster you write the less time you have to "think."

Writing is a heart art, not one of the head. That doesn't mean that all the writing you have been exposed to has come from the heart. Much of the writing you have been exposed to in your life, real estate contracts, insurance forms, etc., have come from an LCM state. But have you sought out those bits of writing for inspiration, guidance, enlightenment? Has what you have read while going over these documents made you feel deeply about something that could be considered positive? Have they positively changed your day, your mood, your life? I think not.

Yes, you can write out of the LCM. It is difficult, time consuming, unfulfilling, and at times painful, and it doesn't usually lead to any positive, inspiring result for the reader, but you can do it.

However, that is not what you are shooting for. You have already had enough pain and despair and you have picked up this book to experience the opposite, which means to continually do so, you will have to focus or continue to focus on writing fast.

How fast? My experience has shown me that your AW will typically express through your CCM at a rate of between 1,200-2,400 words an hour, with an average writing speed of 1,500 words an hour.

What does it mean if you write below that speed? It means that your writing and your writing experience will be held back by inappropriate LCM-based intervention. What then does that translate to? A lousy, frustrating, unfinished experience.

I like to use the analogy of a brand new, shiny car, the exact model and style you always wanted. You already have the keys to that car and the only thing that stands between you and experiencing that car firsthand is a closed garage door. Of course, you can see your car through the windows at the top of the garage door, which makes this entire experience just that much more frustrating, because you can see it very clearly, in all its beauty, but you have not been able to get to it.

Of course, the car is this analogy represents the book inside of you, which is trying to get out. The garage door represents your LCM.

To get at your car and to be able to drive it out of the garage, you have to lift up the garage door not partially up, but all the way up.

If you are trying to write with the garage door only halfway or three-quarters of the way up, that's not enough. You have to lift that garage door all the way up to get the car, in its entirety, all the way out. Then and only then will you feel the peace of accomplishment and full-hearted expression your soul longs for, and that's where the importance of your writing speed comes in. If you're writing at below an average of 1,200 words an hour, you are experiencing inappropriate LCM-based interference, which could lead to a wide range of problems. Remember, even with all of the work you have done up to this point, your LCM still believes that writing and the sharing of it is a painful thing. So it will do anything it can to try to keep you from it or to create a self-fulfilling, failing prophecy in regard to it. That all will clear. But it is still too early in the process to expect a lifetime worth of bad training to be erased. It will take the writing of your book to do that. So until then, it is very important that you keep an eye sharply tuned to the monitoring of your writing speed. How do you do that?

Very simple. For the next few writing sessions, count the number of words you wrote and divide it by the amount of time you wrote? How do you do that? Again, this is very simple. To come up with the approximate number of words you wrote, pick out an average-looking line from what you wrote (not an average-looking sentence). Count the number of words in that line and then write it down. Now count the number of lines you wrote in your session and write that down. Then multiply those two numbers. That will equal the number of words you will have written in the session.

To come up with the number of words per hour you averaged while writing in this session, divide your total by the number of hours you wrote. For example, if you wrote 1,500 words and you did so in one hour, divide 1,500 by one for a total of 1,500. If you wrote 1,500 words during your session but you did so in forty-five minutes, or three quarters of an hour, divide your total by .75, which would equal a writing speed of 2,000 words per hour.

Again, remaining at a speed of at least 1,200 words an hour, the low-water mark, is essential to avoid any unnecessary, oftentimes subliminal hassles as the result of inappropriate LCM intervention.

What if your writing speed falls below 1,200 words an hour? There are several things you can immediately consider.

First, have you been faithfully following the Three Rs of Writing? If not, this could be the source of your problems, especially if you have not been focusing deeply enough on relaxing. If that is the case, go out and buy or use the Creative Writing tape by Potentials Unlimited (available at www.potentialsunlimited.com).

Second, how is your pen working out? Yes, I said "pen." If you're using a pencil or a fine or felt-tipped pen, these will substantially slow your writing speed because they have a tendency to grab onto the fibers of your paper much more than a ballpoint or gel pen. If you need to, this is the time to test drive a new pen or two before continuing.

Third of all, are you experiencing a significant amount of pain in your hand or wrist when you are writing? Even though the source of this pain originates as the result of the LCM-CCM battle, which manifests at the back of your neck and makes it way down your arm through the tightening of tendons and muscles, if you have a structural problem in your wrist or hands, writing in longhand for any length of time may be too much for you. In that case I suggest that you start out by writing in longhand, for say fifteen minutes or so, before switching over to doing your writing on a keyboard. Then every fifteen minutes or so come back over to writing on paper just to ensure you are continually in the necessary CCM-based state while you are doing all of your writing.

Lastly, if none of the alterations or enhancements suggested above make a difference, begin by marking off sections on your writing surface equivalent to the amount of space you would need to write 300 words. Then keep track of the time you are writing and work to write to the end of each section by the time fifteen minutes pass. As simple as this exercise may sound, its results are extreme and I have seen it do more than anything else to quickly bring up the writing speed to an acceptable level.

If you are not already doing so, once you begin writing at the rate of at least 1,200 words an hour, you will feel a shift, a difference, as any inappropriate LCM intervention falls to the wayside.

Ninety-five percent of all the mistakes you could make as a writer are the result of inappropriate LCM intervention. Your enhanced writing speed is essential because when you are writing fast you are doing so at such a rate that you don't have time to think, and, when you're there, you're directly connected with your Source through first your CCM and then your AW, and there's nothing any better than that.

Writing Principle #8

Writing Two Hours a Day, Six Days a Week, You Can Complete a Book in 3-5 Weeks

Do the math. Two hours a day, writing at the pace of 1,500 words per hour, equals 3,000 words per writing session. Six days a week at this pace equals 18,000 words a week. How long then does it take you to write a 70,000-word book, which is somewhere near the average length of an adult American book? Yeah, you get where I'm coming from.

Three hours a day will produce as much as
a man ought to write.

Anthony Trollope

But "Wait," you say, "no one writes a book that fast!"

Old Jack Kerouac used to write a book in three of four days, during which he was continually connected to what he thought at the time to be the Muse. There goes that theory.

> *Please make note that I have completed my book — target date was October 7. The book was actually completed in August.*
> *Deborah Merchant, student, Atlanta, Georgia*

"Okay, okay," you say, "but if you write a book in that short of a period of time it's gonna be crap."

> *Within two months, I had completed my book.*
> *Dr. Nell Rodgers, "Puppet or Puppeteer: Choose the Life You Want to Live" (Awesome Press)*

If we were talking about the processing of a wine or brandy in that short of a period of time, I would have to agree with you. But we're talking about writing, which, because of all the reasons I stated earlier, is best done fast. In fact, as shared earlier, the slower you write the more inappropriate LCM interference and it is that same slow writing speed, one below 1,200 words an hour, which is responsible for 95% of the errors you could make as a writer. To rid yourself of those errors, simply write faster.

Writing Principle #9

Writing on Large Lineless Pieces of Paper Offers Your AW the Surface It Craves to Be Able to Passionately Express Itself

Ninety-five percent of the mistakes you could make with your writing are automatically cured by doing away with inappropriate LCM-based intervention. The other 5% is taken care of by using large lineless pieces of paper to write upon. Why?

First, because the large lineless pieces of paper, obviously void of lines and margins, are more conducive to the expressions of the unconditional, unlimited attributes of your AW.

Secondly, writing on large, lineless pieces of paper offers a writer the perspective necessary to be able to see where he or she has been or is going at all times, which severely limits the chance of a writer's biggest technical problem, redundancy, becoming a part of your experience.

"Are you saying that we have to write in longhand on these large, lineless pieces of paper for the rest of our lives?"

Even though that would probably be a great idea, I realize at the same time that, even though they offer a tremendous amount of convenience on one end, they offer an inconvenience on another end. So I am suggesting that you use them for at least one book if not two. By that time, your atrophied CCM will have hopefully gained enough strength so that it can now stand up to your at-times challenging LCM.

I'm just into proactively. Why do more drafts and make writing any harder than it needs to be by utilizing obsolete or just plain ineffective methods? Get in an

Sample poster board showing notes in the margins

AW-connected state. Write fast and do so on large pieces of lineless paper. Stay there for two hours. Then repeat and repeat; repeat sessions such as this one until you are finished writing your book. Not only will any of the mistakes you could have potentially experienced be severely limited, but you will end up with a finished rough draft, oozing with the depth, direction, passion, and heart that most authors, even world-famous ones, often go through several drafts to try to find and then inject.

If I haven't already said enough on this topic, why do you think your kids, who are still living through their CCMs, want to write on the walls? Are they not the biggest, lineless, most unconditional spaces in the house? And they are wanting to express through their…

"CCMs."

Right. And for you to be able to express completely and successfully, you have to do so through…

"My CCM."

Correct again.

Why then do you feel that William Faulkner, an author ahead of his time, wrote on the walls of his house as well? Or why was it that internationally recognized genius Walt Disney did all of his plotting and planning on large line-less sheet of paper as well?

A word to the wise is sufficient.

Writing Principle #10

You Are Doing Your Best Writing
When You Don't Know Where You Are Going

The part of you that is conditional and thus needs to know is your…

"LCM."

Right.

So, if you are maintaining your writing speed at such a level that you are outrunning any LCM-based intervention, your LCM will not…

"Know where you are going."

Correct. So now do you see that if you are writing really fast that is a good thing and, as a result of writing at that speed, your LCM will not know where you are going, which is a good thing?

"I guess so," reluctantly answers your LCM.

Again, your rate of speed during the writing process is essential to your success. It not only eliminates unnecessary mistakes by limiting LCM self-sabotage but it also guarantees a successful experience by doing so. Thus, a symptom such as your LCM not knowing where you are going, which is indicative of being in the right space doing the right thing, is a good thing, is it not?

If at first the idea is not absurd, then there
is no hope for it.

Albert Einstein

In essence, the writing of a book very much mirrors the reading of a book and your AW knows this and uses it to both of your advantage.

If you pick up a book and begin reading it, and by page fourteen you know exactly what the author is going to share and how the book is going to end, do you continue to read it?

"No."

If in the same vein you sat down to write a book and knew exactly how each detail of it was going to be laid out all the way through to the end, would you have the same zest for writing it?

"No."

So not knowing where you are going is a good thing then because it coaxes you though to the completion of a project?

"I guess so."

When writing your book, your priorities will shift substantially from writing for a result to writing for the process. As a result, as you stretch out onto your pillow of unconditional acceptance and appreciation provided by your connection with the Source, you will be motivated less by wanting to get the book done and instead wanting to come back to the pen and paper over and over and over again to get that love bump you will be used to. As a result, you will no longer struggle with caring where the story is going or with who is doing what, which is a good thing.

Don't worry now, not knowing where you are going is a good thing. In fact, to a person, all of the students with whom I work are usually concerned when I offer them the opportunity to read for the initial time the first book they wrote using this method.

"I'm sure it's going to suck," they all say. "I mean, I don't even know what I wrote about," which ends up being a good thing. The less understanding of a topic you have while writing a book, the less LCM intervention, the better the book.

When the language lends itself to me, when it comes and submits, when it surrenders and says—'I am yours, darling'—that's the best part.

Maya Angelou

Much to their delight, all come away more than pleasantly surprised with their result after reading their works for the first time, the positive results of which can be attributed to Not Knowing Where They Are Going.

Part of the Not Knowing Where You Are Going during this method comes directly as the result of connecting with your archetypes.

From a literary standpoint, I define archetypes as *"symbolic representations of universal meanings."* To be more blunt, if your writing is leading you off in the direction of fiction, your archetypes will be defined as your characters. If you are writing nonfiction, your archetypes will be embodied in the essence of the themes, theories, and/or voice or tone that make up your book. At their deepest level, archetypes are the deliverers of your Divine, personal message, who literally write whatever you are composing for you. Yes, they literally push the pen in your hand along, where they want it to go, writing whatever it is that they want you to write. Even though being in this Divine sort of connection can make you feel so much less important than your ego wants you to feel, it is a whole lot easier this way.

I can believe anything, provided it is incredible.

Oscar Wilde

So that your LCM can better understand this experience, thus better understand what is going on, and so not mistakenly interrupt your writing process, I want to better clarify for you the two types of archetypes that could surface.

Usually the first type of archetype to surface during this method is the Transitional Archetype (TA). These archetypes exist for one purpose only: to educate you through the removal of your own biases. The TA's purpose is to help you remove whatever biases may exist (most of which are against yourself or your abilities) so that you can go along to wherever your writing leads you.

TAs typically appear in your mind as an image of someone you love and trust and rarely, if ever (unless you are writing an autobiographical book), end up being a part of your book. Once their job is done–Poof–they're gone, never to be seen in this form again, their absence making room for the second type of archetype, the Primary Archetype (PA). So don't freak out if your mom

Success Story by John Hodgkinson

From: John Hodgkinson, Lakeside, California
To: Tom Bird

Tom taught us the concept of finding our Transformation Archetype. On day three, we started the morning off with a few brief words and then we were turned over to our TA. For the next three hours I had an exchange with Tal'man that revealed a great deal about physical life. Questions were answered dealing with utilizing the senses for meditation and also for writing. The questions were all prephysical-based and the knowledge that I received about the Universe was unreal. I wrote well over two to three thousand words. I was on a roll, and my hand was really tired at the end.

"This experience inspired me to no end and has changed my life forever. It broadened my belief and understanding that we do have guides, angels, masters, etc., waiting there for our beck and call. My TA is there for my undivided attention anytime I'm ready to finish completing my lifetime work. He's there every step of the way with my writing. What I have learned is that I have to ask all the questions. But I can tap into him whenever I need to. That includes driving down the road.

"Let me share an interesting story with you as an example of this. One morning when climbing into the shower I had a strange thought. 'Don't drive in the fast lane today.' Weird, I thought. What's that all about? I ignored it. While driving to work, as I do every day, I drove in the fast lane. Halfway to work, I hit a divot in the road and blew out my front left tire. After pulling over to the right side of the highway, I realized I needed to walk a mile up the road to find a phone. While walking along the highway, I decided to invoke my TA. I kept saying, 'Okay, Tal'man or God, whichever wants to answer, what's the message behind this flat tire?'

"I got all the way to the gas station at the next off ramp and made a call to Triple A. They asked me to meet the driver at the car so I began walking back. 'Hey, guys, what's up? You haven't answered my question. I'm invoking the big three and you're not answering.'

"Moments later, I happened to look down and spot a nickle and a penny. I picked them up and held them in the palm of my hand. 'Okay,' I said, 'what's the message you're trying to give me in the six cents? Oops,' I said with a laugh. 'I get it. *Use your Sixth Sense.*'

or someone else like her seems to magically appear when you first start writing your book. Relax. Unless you are writing something of a straight autobiographical nature, she has probably just shown up in your mind to help you better love yourself.

> *I met my TA in one of Tom's seminars of The Writers' Success Series on March 10, 2001. (Yes, the spring before the world exploded.) The Native American-looking, with blue eyes and long black hair, dude's name was/is 'Magic.' (Clumsy sentence, but you get the picture.)*
> *Frances Ring, Student, Boca Raton, Florida*

PAs are the bearers of messages much different from those of their counterparts, the TAS. PAs are the delivers of the messages found at the heart of your writing, and they literally do the writing for you.

So I just wanted your LCM to be able to differentiate between TAs and PAs, so that it knows where it is going when You Don't Know You Are Going.

> *She, Cara, was also the first Primary Archetype (PA). In many ways, she was me, but clearly stating what I/she wanted to accomplish. She had my wishes and hopes, but she could actualize them; she could have all the good luck. She had problems, but she could work on them. She introduced me to Billy Joe. He introduced both of us to Barb, who introduced all of us to Psue.*
> *Cass Brady, student, Atlanta, Georgia*

Writing Principle #11

You Are Giving Yourself a Chance to Do Your Best Writing When You Do Not Read What You Have Written Until You Have Completed Your Book

Yeah, what I am saying is to refrain from reading your writing until you have completely finished it. Why?

First of all, reading your material brings forth your LCM, and we want to keep as far away from that as possible during the writing process.

If you stop to read any portion of your material during the writing process, you stop writing and you do what?

"Read."

Reading in this manner then...

"Stops or slows the writing process."

Correct. And doing so would do what?

"Stop the flow the CCM and bring out the LCM."

Right, which would...

"Bring the writing to a halt."

Yes, and you would end up right where?

"I began before the reading of this book."

And before you began reading this book you were a...

"Frustrated writer."

And you want to avoid doing what at all costs?

"Going back to that place."

Correct.

Second, it's best to wait until your CCM has gained considerable strength through the writing of your book and can stand up to what may be the unmatched strength of your LCM. In that way, you will be keeping your book from being judged harshly and potentially unfairly by the

LCM and until its time, or your LCM may do what to your writing?

"Destroy it."

Right.

Writing Principle #12

Hold All Research to the End of Your Book

In the same vein as the above, stopping to research facts, figures, dates, descriptions, or whatever during the writing process interrupts the flow of your AW through your CCM. And with each interruption it is subjected to, it stands a chance of being shut down for good. Making time to research while writing simply isn't worth the risk.

Plus, my experience has shown me that over 90% of the information collected before the writing of a book (from here on referred to as pre-writing research) does not end up surfacing in the final draft of the book. In essence then, pre-writing research equates to socially accepted procrastination.

Yes, I know that you have heard many an author claim they had researched for dozens of years before finally sitting down to write their books. But that still doesn't mean that they couldn't have written the same book much, much faster and possibly even better if they had shared the belief that there was an already-written book inside of them just trying to get out, which is what the entire premise of this work, my teaching, and my success has been about for nearly a quarter of a century.

If they had believed that that had been the case, they would have modified their system to work in a similar fashion to the method I have been employing and sharing with my students for so long. They would have simply plugged into whatever book that they felt coming out of them; adjusted their method of writing to best suit the needs of their AWs, who are the true authors of all great books anyway; and, as the book was spilling out of them, they would have just noted gaps in their understanding of facts, figures, names, dates, descriptions, or whatever, which they could come back to and address at a later time through what I refer to as post-writing research.

I'm sure that you can see how this approach to research can significantly shorten the writing time of any book from taking several years to just a few months, if unnecessary pre-writing research is eliminated all together.

As well, a myriad of problems arise if an author spends too long in the company of one project. Remember that an author's most valuable asset is his or her own voice expressed in a passionate way.

Even the slowest-growing person changes substantially over a long period of time, which means as well that his or her voice alters too. So if it takes you a long time to write a book, you can just bet on the fact that several different, potentially conflicting voices will be present in your finished version.

Writing fast at all times keeps the LCM in its place. It eliminates any chance that you will have your book inappropriately influenced by a formerly defeating behavior pattern. Holding off doing your research until the completion of a writing project plays a big part, because doing so does not allow your LCM to have any form of negative influence during your AW's crucial time of writing.

"But what happens if you are doing a book based on interviews or something like that?"

Good question. In all cases, release whatever book is in you. Let it show you what it is and what it needs. In some cases, you will find that a book needs the addition, through post-writing research, of a few dates, names, and figures. Others will need some developed description. Others, such as a book of interviews, will come out in a skeletal fashion, offering not much more than an Introduction and a developed outline of itself. In either case, when you go back to do your post-writing research, no matter how skimpy or advanced it may be, you will know exactly what it is that you are looking for. You can rest assured that the process will not take any longer than absolutely necessary and that your final version will comprise, on all levels, your finest effort possible. Period.

Writing Principle #13

All Great and Effective Writing Is the Result of a Direct Interaction with the AW

Through the years, I have had many students receive the impression from my teaching that what I was offering them would only work with so-called "creative" projects such as the writing of fiction. In every case what they refused to understand was that all writing projects are potentially "creative" and that the job of writing is to communicate.

Now some persons who write fail miserably at this, of course, such as those who write the majority of contracts, insurance agreements, or whatever. All they communicate is essential information housed in a very frustrating, hard-to-understand, oftentimes-impossible-to-even-read-let-alone-digest form.

"But that's what documents such as those are meant to do, right?"

No.

The goal of all writing is to communicate, not confuse and frustrate, and certainly not put someone to sleep. Just because a legacy of failure in this regard has been in place for potentially hundreds of years doesn't mean that it needs to be extended and honored through your work.

Let me offer you a few examples of this.

A number of years ago I was contacted by a professor from the Nursing Department at the University of Tennessee. I had recently appeared at the university. She had a scheduling conflict and as a result was unable to attend my lectures, so she was contacting me to see if I would be able to work with her on an individual basis.

Her situation was this. She and a colleague had written a book on the spiritual aspects of nursing, which they hoped to have published as a textbook and distributed nationally through colleges and universities.

She paid me to review her manuscript and then offer my assessment, which I did. When she called at our prearranged consultation time, I began our conversation by asking her how honest she wanted me to be about the quality of her book.

"Absolutely honest," she replied.

"Okay, then," I replied. "The bad news is that the book sucks, but the good news is that I found about five sentences that actually work. Of course, all we then have to do is rewrite the book from the same frame of mind you were in when you wrote those five sentences and then you'll have a great book."

"But it's a textbook," she responded.

"Just because all your other colleagues wrote boring books doesn't mean that you have to follow in their foot-steps," I challenged.

To make a long story shorter, I worked with this professor for a considerable period of time just to get her

Success Story by Lorraine Justice

From: Lorraine Justice, Atlanta, Georgia
To: Tom Bird

As a university professor, I'm accustomed to writing for my discipline of industrial design. I write and present papers all over the world, always staying within the bounds of professional acceptability. But on a personal level something was missing.

I wanted to write about other issues that meant a lot to me, but I couldn't get the words out. (This is not good when you have a Ph.D. in communications!) I realized after my first class with Tom, at Emory University, that he was right; there is an author within who I had not yet accessed.

After I began working with Tom, I couldn't stop myself from writing. The words came out in a steady stream. The flow seemed to come through me, rather than from me. My words were intense, passionate, unusual, and had much more importance for me than anything else I'd written.

My muse appeared at 5:00 in the morning or 8:00 in the evening, whenever I sat down to write. I was connected. I also knew when that connection broke and the words were inauthentic. My pen rose on its own from the paper when the muse was gone.

I know now that I write from a different place and the communication is authentic. I put words together in ways I hadn't dreamed of prior to working with Tom. The writing became cathartic, too, and I began to heal

parts of me that felt raw and ragged for years. I know I will continue to write. I am so grateful to Tom for having the courage to carry his unorthodox message on writing to others. He is a gift."

heart to come through her writing. Once that was accomplished, she then rewrote her book from that perspective and then she submitted it to a collection of academic publishers who published her sort of text. Within a few weeks, three of them contacted her to offer contracts for her work, which was a great thing. However, what was even more confirming for me was the fact that each one of them who offered her a contract conveyed basically the same information to her: that they had each been looking for a book like hers for quite some time, but that each manuscript they received was written in a dull, dry, and boring textbook manner, which was exactly the opposite of what they felt would be appropriate for a work focusing on the spiritual aspects of nursing.

A man will turn over half a library
to make one book.

Samuel Johnson

In another case, I was once working with a tax attorney. Is there any more of a LCM-based profession than a tax attorney? Well, anyway, he wanted to write a novel and began to do so under my guidance, which all of sudden led him to an increased value at work. Why? Simply because what he was opening up through the writing of his novel allowed him to transfer that same something (AW) over to his writing of briefs at work. The result? He began to receive a higher appreciation in the workplace because his writing there began to better convey his message, no matter how LCM-based the content he had to work with may have been.

All great and effective writing is the result of a direct interaction with the AW.

Writing Principle #14

Always Conclude a Writing Session in the Midst of a Section or Chapter

Why? Because if you conclude a writing session at the end of a chapter or section you also bring to a conclusion your flow, at least for that portion of your writing, which makes it ten times as difficult to begin writing the next day because you will have to create a flow to attach on to. It's better and easier to tap into a flow that already exists as opposed to trying to create one each session. Avoiding having to create a new flow every session will also enable you to limit the amount of dead writing in your work, which is sure to exist during the time when you may be warming up in an attempt to establish or find an AW-based flow.

So the ultimate scenario would feature you connecting with your AW, writing well, and concluding a writing session in the midst of a chapter and/or section. Then reconnecting with your Author Within just before you begin the next session. Then, after doing so, rewriting the last 20-30 words you wrote the time before, which would tune you right back in to the momentum and tone you had the session before.

Always conclude a writing session in the middle of a section or chapter.

Writing Principle #15

It Is Essential to Reserve Time to
Get to Know, Love and then Embrace
Your Own Unique and Brilliant Creative Voice

How much time does the above equate to?

I would budget the amount of time it takes you to write your first book using this method. Oh yeah, that would mean avoiding the reading of anything other than magazines and newspapers and anything you may have to read for work or for a class you may be taking. Other than that, no books.

"What?"

Yes, you heard me correctly. Don't read any books during this small, but very important window in your life, other than the ones you have to read for work or for a class.

When I want to read a novel I write one.

Benjamin Disraeli

"But why," you vehemently object.

Hey, as a result of my many years of teaching, I knew many things about you even before you picked up this book. I knew that you had wanted to write for a substantial period of time. I knew that you may have tried to shake this desire on many occasions, but weren't able to. I knew that your momentum to pursue this task has grown every day. I knew that you may have even attempted to write a book or two on your own, or maybe you actually did complete some writing, but you weren't, for whatever reason, satisfied with the result. I know that your AW had visited you on several occasions and everything seemed to work just right with your writing, but that you weren't able to identify exactly what it was that happened and as a result you were unable to emulate it on a consistent basis. I also knew that there is an extremely high probability that you like to read a lot, which, of course, is the result of you borrowing someone else's AW connection to sublimate your own inability to connect. All of that will change, of course, once you start connecting on your own using this method. In fact, you may have already begun feeling the difference. You may already know the difference I am referring to–the one that draws you less to the AW connections of others through the reading of their books, and instead continually leads you off in the direction of your own connection through your writing. This, of course, will annually save you hundreds of dollars in book purchases while potentially adding extra money to your pocket through publication.

"Okay fine, but why discontinue reading right now and for such a long period of time?"

It's not a long period of time. In the entire spectrum of things, the time period I am referring to is a single drop of rain in a downpour.

To read too many books is harmful.

Mao Tse-Tung

"Okay. But why sever myself from something I love so much at any time?"

Why do you think?

"Because through doing the type of reading your refer to would cause me to emulate the styles of other writers?"

That's true, but that not the answer I am looking for.

"Okay, ummm, well, I don't know why else then."

Let me ask you this then: How does your LCM learn?

"Ummmmm."

Correct. Through rote and repetition.

"Oh, okay."

What does that have to do with this entire process?

"I don't know."

Let me ask you this, has your LCM ever had enough uninterrupted time with your AW to allow it to familiarize itself with your own creative voice so that it can finally accept it?

"Obviously not."

Correct. Never has your LCM been offered the chance to get to know your AW and its brilliant and creative voice. As a result of the fact that your LCM automatically rejects that which it does not recognize, it has been rejecting your AW and your own unique, special voice. Got it?

"Yep."

So to give your LCM the chance it needs to get to know this wonderfully expressive and Divine part of yourself, you need to do what?

"Reserve time for it to get to know, love, and then embrace my own unique and brilliant creative voice."

Writing Principle #16

Two Drafts Is All It Takes to Complete the Writing of Your Heart's Desire

Two drafts–that's it.

You may have seen the movie Finding Forrester with Sean Connery. If you haven't seen it, I highly recommend that you watch it, because it's maybe the only movie on writing that at least moderately depicts, in a functional way, both the craft and those who participate in it.

In the movie, Connery is a reclusive famous author who changed people's lives with his writing and then disappeared after his first book. Accidentally though (even though there are no accidents), he is discovered by a young man in the same neighborhood as his in the Bronx, who wants to, of course, write.

Eventually they become each other's mentors. The young man teaches Connery about himself and life while Sean counsels the young man on writing.

There is a scene in the movie that accurately depicts what I am referring to with the statement from above. In the scene, the young man and Connery are facing each other across a desk. Between them lie two relics of type-writers. Connery commands the young man to begin writing, which he is unable to do. So Connery demon-strates for the young man what he means and he begins typing, all the while he is still carrying on a conversation with his pupil, saying something along the lines of the following.

"The first draft is all heart," he says, as he continues allowing his fingers to dance across the keys. "The second draft is where you use your head."

Exactly.

The first draft should be written completely and totally from the AW. The second and final draft is where you utilize the skills of your LCM, under the watchful and patient eye of your strengthened CCM, of course.

If you offer what is needed through your composition of the first draft, which is a direct, monogamous connection with your AW, there will be no need for extensive follow-up drafts, which are no more than attempts to find the heart in your writing that you had somehow left out in your first run-through. If the heart is there in your first draft, then so is the depth and direction necessary to form a book. And if they're all there, then all you have to do is revise your material along the lines I suggest later and you will be done.

There is also another reason that you want to avoid going beyond a second and final draft. Not only is it extremely inefficient to do so, but the more drafts beyond the second one that you go into the more frustrated, at least subconsciously, you will become with the book, which will show in how you attack it (yes, from the second draft on you will be attacking it).

Two drafts is all it takes to complete the writing of your heart's desire.

Writing Principle #17

You Don't Have to Be Highly Educated, or Even Proficient, in Spelling, Punctuation, and Grammar to Be a Successful Writer

If that weren't the case, every English teacher/professor and librarian would be a best-selling author, and then where would we be?

No. The key to good or even great writing, all successful, communicative writing, directly springs from your ability to tap into your heart (AW) and then release it through your CCM.

If you're anything like me, from year to year to year I slept through those sessions on grammar, punctuation, and spelling. Never before had I run into material so dry and boring and which appeared to be such a waste of my time. That's not to say that learning to spell, punctuate properly, and master grammar is a waste of anyone's time. Nothing could be further from the truth.

I am the Roman Emperor, I am above grammar.

Sigismund

However, since the learning of it far preceded any application of it through my writing, I just never saw a need for it. And then because of my long, drawn-out exposure to it, when I was finally given the chance to do some writing, it appeared as if punctuation, spelling, and grammar were at the core of any good writing, which wasn't even close to being what I discovered as the truth. Sure they are important, but they are nothing unless the writing they are formed around has been released passionately and directly from one's heart.

So yes, they are important, but they are not what is at the true essence of the writing your AW will do. They will help to refine that essence. They will help to better communicate it, but they are not that essence.

So, if you're anything like me, and your grasp of the technical factors of writing is a bit remedial, so what? You can buff that up with a little bit more study in that area, a copy editor, or grammar- and spell-check. But nobody, absolutely no one, will ever be able to replace the special AW gift you bring into this world through your CCM and the AW's unique, one-of-kind expressive voice.

Moving On

If you have effectively moved through your work with the aforementioned principles, you are now ready to move on to the release of your book, which has been forever waiting to be birthed. Through it, you will be able to see just how much you have learned, how much you have grown, and how brilliant, wonderful, and Divine you are. Enjoy.

Committing to Your Journey

ONTRARY TO WHAT YOU MAY HAVE BEEN TOLD OR MAY have thought about yourself, you don't lack commitment. Not only have you progressed from grade to grade, graduated from schools, held down jobs, paid off loans, possibly even successfully raised children, but you have remained true to yourself through the completion of the exercises that have preceded this chapter. You have not given up on your purpose, and, most importantly, you have made time to do something about it. Bravo!

You are very brave and very committed. From my perspective, you don't have to commit more. Moving forward, you simply need to commit more wisely, which means completing the following.

The Contract

There is one common denominator amongst all of the commitments you have followed through on in your life. That common denominator is an agreement that you have entered into, either formally or informally, with yourself and most probably with an outside source as well. Some form of contractual agreement is always the difference between success and failure. So wouldn't it make sense that if you wanted to succeed at the writing of a book that you should enter into a contract as well?

As far as this contract is concerned, you can write it in longhand, type it out, whatever, as long as it is committed to paper, copied, and distributed in the manner suggested. All of this, including mailing it, will cost you less than five dollars and take you less than a few hours, travel time included.

The need for this contract is very real. You may have been talking about writing a book for years and your LCM has heard every one of your claims, which up to this point have been nothing more than empty promises. As a result, your LCM doesn't believe you when you say you're going to write a book. Can you blame it? All that it has experienced up to this point are a bunch of empty promises. Remember, your LCM has led you to every success in your life and we need to get it on your side now so it can lead you to the success you seek as a writer. But frankly, it has grown callous to your claims. It needs something firm, tangible, a document to verify that you are actually going to do something this time. That's where the contract comes in. Do it and you will, in all likelihood, succeed. Avoid it and, in all likelihood, you won't.

Your Written Commitment—Signed and Dated

Here are a few hints in regard to the direction your contract should take.

- Your agreement needs to be signed and dated.
- It should convey as much passion as possible.

- It should showcase a general statement of purpose, which basically answers the question, "What you are promising to do?"

- A timeframe in which you will complete your book needs to be included. For your purposes, writing six days a week and two hours a day at a writing speed of 1,500 words an hour, give yourself five weeks, which, of course, translates to 30 days of actual writing.

- Clearly state what it is that you will receive on a daily basis if you complete your writing goals and what it is that you will not get if you don't. This will do more than anything else to get your LCM on your side. Make sure that you are not being wimpy and weak here. Take away that glass of wine at the end of the day if you don't complete your writing assignment or that bit of chocolate after dinner that you love so much, or keep yourself from having any coffee at all. All you need to miss is one session and the LCM will quickly learn that when you write you get good things and when you don't you experience pain. Thus, with its primary purpose being to lead you away from pain, your LCM will immediately reverse its approach to writing and begin leading you to it as opposed to leading you away from it.

- Once your contract is complete, make seven copies of it. Keep the first copy for yourself and ensure that this document is in view each and every time you write. Send the second copy to me at **TomBird@TomBird.com**, which will comprise a formal rite of passage to your LCM. Then take the next three copies and send one each off to three persons who you would consider tough love specialists. You know, the ones who would remind you the rest of your days if you fell short of your goal. For God's sake, why send to them? Because their presence will do more to motivate your LCM to keep you on track than anything else. The last two copies? Send to two people who love you unconditionally, who won't be anywhere near as motivating because they'll love you whether you succeed or not, and as a result your LCM won't be motivated nearly as much by them.

Once you have completed this essential task, turn to the next section.

Here are some sample agreements I have included for your convenience.

The great thing in this world is not so much where we are, but in what direction we are moving.

Oliver Wendell Holmes

Individual Agreement #1

On this seventh (7th) day of October in the year 2005, I (Author), do enter into this contract willingly and with full knowledge of what is expected of me by me. I write this contract in order to commit myself to writing a book, a book that is presently inside of me now. I will complete this book by Thanksgiving of the year 2005. I do understand the necessity of this contract binding me to a commitment of writing.

I will reserve two hours daily, six days a week, to write.

I will remove all distractions. I will set boundaries for those near and dear to me and ask them to respect those boundaries, so that I may have uninterrupted time.

I will do relaxing exercises before writing, while writing, and after writing.

I will allow my thoughts and feelings to flow freely onto blank index cards.

I will post my results on a bulletin board on the wall above my desk.

I will make a list of all that I would like to have and do.

I will break them into daily, weekly actions.

On a daily basis, I will reward myself with a cigarette and an O'Doules, (even if it is 10 o'clock in the morning) on the patio.

When I have made a completion of one step, I will treat myself and my children to a full-course lobster meal at a restaurant.

When I have finished my final copy and have sent it off to the Literary Agent, I will travel to Sedona and spend the day, complete with a picnic lunch of my favorite foods, on the back site of Oak Creek Canyon. I will take pictures and rejoice in my favorite place. I will take my son and daughter, if possible.

I gladly and willingly and most excitedly do sign this contract.

_____   _____
Author   Date

Individual Agreement #2

On this day of November 24, 2005, I hereby openly make clear my intentions to finally complete the book which has been keeping me up for years, and to start on my heartfelt career as a self-supporting author.

My plan of action will be this:

A) I will rise every morning at least ninety minutes before I usually get up, follow The Three Rs of Writing to put me in the proper mood, and then follow the appropriate directions from *You Were Born to. . . Write*.

B) By doing this, I plan to have my first book by January 24, 2006.

C) By no later than January 25, 2006, I will begin individually contacting literary agents.

D) With this plan in mind, I will land the proper agent for my book by no later than February 27, 2006.

E) Any revenues raised from the sale of my first book, or any that follow, will be placed in a special bank account established for the sole purpose of accumulating enough money for me to resign from my position at the bank and go to work on my writing full time.

F) As far as my routine and writing are concerned, I will stick with the aforementioned routine six days a week, each morning—moving from book to book—until I have earned enough to resign from my position. At that time, I will then follow the same routine with The Three Rs of Writing and devote myself to painting a minimum of five hours a day, with time put aside each day for the sales of my work.

I realize the importance of each person to whom I have sent a copy of this contract, and I call upon each one to police my heartfelt efforts in whatever way he or she chooses. If at any time I fall short of any of the goals listed above, and their corresponding deadlines, I hereby promise to treat each person who received a copy of this contract to a dinner at his or her favorite restaurant.

God is with us all.

Bert Zimpa

Individual Agreement #3

July 7, 2005—I, Jan Smith, will begin following the dream of writing a book.

To make this dream happen, I will faithfully stay connected to my deepest inspiration by following The Three Rs of Writing and writing each morning.

The information that I gather from these sessions, I will use to guide me spiritually, financially, and logistically.

By no later than August 7, 2005, I will have completed my rough draft.

By August 17, 2005, I will have begun working on my revision.

I will have my book completed and ready for submission to literary agents by no later than October 10, 2005.

I will continue to follow my routine with my morning writing, and reserve time each day.

To this goal, I devote all my heart and soul. May the results which are achieved become a reminder to many that our dreams come true. All that is needed is a little faith, consistent effort, and, most of all, that ultimate of all connections flowing through our life each day.

For each of you who has been chosen to receive a copy of this contract, you have carte blanche to check on my progress, per the above dates and terms, whenever you see fit. If I am caught falling behind on any, I will gladly donate one free hour of yard work to each and every one of you receiving this agreement.

May God guide all of our actions.

Jan Smith

Getting Started and Your Last Minute Checklist Before Beginning

OKAY, LET'S GO OVER YOUR CHECKLIST TO MAKE SURE THAT you have everything you need for your grand and glorious journey.

1. All of your contracts, especially the one meant to go to me, should have been sent out.

2. A weekly writing schedule of no less than two hours a day, six days a week, should have been arranged.

3. Those in your life or with whom you share a home or office, or wherever you write, should have been warned about the necessary private time that is needed for your writing and warned that you will enforce your rights in this regard at all costs.

Here are the things to keep in mind at all times in regard to your writing experience. Read over the following at least once a week, unless you run into a problem or a stoppage with your writing. In that case, immediately turn to this page and read over the following to see which of the suggestions you have innocently forgotten to implement. Put that procedure back into practice, all will then be healed, and get back to your writing.

1. Always write as fast as you can.
2. Always precede any writing, or reading of your writing, by first following the Three Rs of Writing.
3. Do not edit, review, or read your work as you are writing.
4. Leave gaps for any bits of information or facts that you may need to research later.
5. Consistently pat yourself on the back, with some sort of reward, after the completion of each successful writing session.
6. If any potentially distracting thoughts pop into your mind, dump them into a narrow right-hand column on the right side of each of your pieces of paper.

Do or do not, there is no try.

Yoda

---

7. Work on your writing two hours a day, six days a week, no matter what happens.
8. Make sure to never conclude a writing session at the end of a chapter or section.

9. Remember to warm up at the beginning of each writing session by recopying the last 20-30 words that you wrote during your most recent session.

10. Just let the words fly out of you, allowing your AW to take you and your writing wherever it is that you are both destined to go.

11. Outside of required reading for your job or for a class, and magazines and newspapers, don't do any reading while completing your book or screenplay.

12. No matter how much preparatory work we have done up to this point, you'll still not know where you are going with your writing from day to day. Remember, this is your AW's way of keeping you interested.

A Few Last-Minute Insights to Keep in Mind that We Haven't Yet Covered

1. The writing of any major project usually starts off slowly. In fact, it is not unusual for some switching back and forth by your AW in regard to the point of view employed and whether the first or third person is used. Until you both get used to each other, don't allow any early sluggishness to rattle you. Your connection will smooth out eventually.

2. Whenever Thomas Edison used to run into a problem with one of his inventions, he used to take a catnap. You see, Edison believed that when

one slept, his or her soul left the body and went to a higher level of consciousness, and then it came back and re-entered the body upon re-awakening, bringing back with it whatever information it was lacking or needed to know. You may find Edison's theory helpful with your writing. You may even find yourself starting to fall asleep during your writing sessions. This is not because your writing is boring. This is happening because your AW is reaching for a higher level of understanding, which it can't quite reach while you are in a waking state. So if you feel as if you want to go to sleep during a writing session, allow yourself to do so. Just put your head down on your desk and nod off. In no time at all, you will wake back up with a renewed vigor and point of view that wasn't there before falling asleep.

3. To help ease the concerns of your LCM, you may want to use the last five minutes of each writing session to jot down where your CCM sees you going the next day. That way, with a roadmap of at least the next day's destination squarely in front of it, your LCM won't feel so lost and out of control.

4. You may also want to reserve the last ten minutes or so before you retire for the evening to do some brainstorming on paper. Doing so especially helps to prime your AW for really taking off the next morning. In fact, after arising, if you experience any sluggishness at all with your writing, you will find that doing this usually cures you of it.

5. Since the side of us that we tie-in to when writing affects us and those we are connected most closely

with, it is not unusual for a person to experience a short period of time, shortly after beginning on a book, when the poop in other areas of his or her life seems to be hitting the fan. If that begins to happen to you, don't overreact. Everything and everyone will calm down in a few days as they adjust to the massive amount of new energy you're allowing to enter into your life, through your writing.

6. If you happen to fall off of your writing schedule for a few days, don't plan to jump back in where you left off and go. There may be some personal stuff that has to be released first, through your writing, before you can do so.

7. Your project will end on its own. You will also be given very little advance notice of when this will happen. Just a few minutes before it concludes is usually the norm. The reason for this short notice is so that your LCM will not have time to come out and screw up your execution.

8. Remember that all you need to know, you already know, and all you need to have, you already have in your possession. To remind yourself of this fact, all you have to do is to look back through this book at all that you have already accomplished.

Okay, it's time to begin. I will get you started, but from this point forward it will be you, your AW, as it comes through your CCM, doing all the work.

Step 1: Get into your AW/CCM-connected state.

Step 2: Pull out a piece of your chosen writing surface, and in the center of it, write the working title of your book.

Step 3: Allow yourself to completely free-associate any thoughts or feelings, whether they are directly tied to what you will be writing or not, by releasing them onto the lineless piece of paper before you, and making sure to circle each expression and then connect each circled item to the nearest item to it with a straight line. Remember just to allow these expressions to fly out of you as fast as you can.

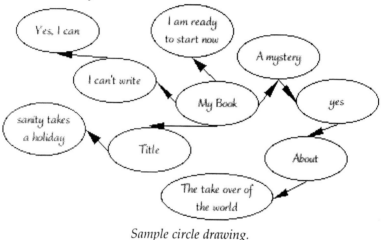

Sample circle drawing.

Step 4: Sometime in between 8-15 minutes of doing this you will feel a very strong and consistent stream of consciousness coming through you. When you feel this, go to another piece of lineless paper and, while following the rules above, just allow this, which will be your book, to come streaming out of you. Stay with this stream of AW consciousness for an average of two consecutive hours before reconnecting with it the next day, the next day, and however many days it takes after that until your book, all on its own, comes to a conclusion.

Your Second and Final Draft

B Y NOW, YOU SHOULD HAVE COMPLETED THE FIRST DRAFT OF your book. Congratulations, over 85% of what you set out to do is now done.

During this final draft of your book you will be replacing the time you had carved out of your schedule for writing with the following steps. Even though these activities are vastly different from the steps you have taken with your writing up to this point, it is still important that you make sure to follow The Three Rs of Writing before beginning any session. Also keep in mind that each of the following will take up to several days to complete. When you are done with these steps you will be finished with your book.

An Essential Point to Keep in Mind During this Draft

Somewhere during this last draft, the idea for your next book will pop out. By all means, do not ignore it. In fact, when it does appear, begin reserving one-third of the time you have allotted to the reworking of your manuscript for the releasing of your second book on the large pieces of paper.

Begin doing so by using the circle drawing exercise described earlier. Then just let it flow.

Reserving time to release your next book is essential because it counterbalances the stiffness of the LCM-based type of activities that follow, enabling you to glide through them with much greater ease.

So don't forget, when that next book shows up, devote a certain portion of your time each day to letting it out.

Noting and Then Making Structural Changes

The revision and review of your manuscript begins with you entering into your AW-connected state and then reading through your book, noting all major changes you would like to make to your work.

Major changes are defined as any alterations, rearrangements, subtractions, or additions that directly affect the general theme or direction of what you have already written. This does not include grammatical changes and/or the correction of typographical mistakes . The easiest way I have found to note these types of changes is to write down any suggestions I may have on Post-It Notes and then place the notes on my chosen writing surface wherever I am suggesting my changes be made.

After you have completed the above, go through and make whatever major changes that need to be made in your manuscript. You may have to, of course, use several

Sample poster board showing notes in the margins

other pieces of your chosen writing surface to do so. It may take several days to complete this task. Don't move on to the next step until you have fully completed this one.

Post-Writing Research

Fill in all the research gaps you left in your manuscript. After you have completed this task, move on to the next step.

The Colors of the Rainbow

No one will ever know the purpose and meaning of your work better than you. With that in mind, you and you alone will be in charge of fine-tuning your manuscript. To do so, you will need a pack of four different colored highlighters.

In regard to your highlighters, we will be using them to make six separate sweeps through your manuscript. Each sweep may comprise more than one session.

On the first pass-through, designate one highlighter for marking all your action verbs.

On the second sweep, take another marker and highlight all your passive verbs.

On the third pass-through, use the last two markers to highlight all your adjectives and adverbs.

These three sweeps through your manuscript may take days. If you are confused and unsure on these different forms of language, this is a good time to go back and brush up on your grammar.

Once you have completed your highlighting, on the third sweep, go through your manuscript and focus solely on each of your action verbs. With each and every action verb, ask yourself if you are using the most appropriate and expressive verb possible. If you have not done so, change whatever you have written to the appropriate verb.

After you have completed your work with the action verbs, on the fifth sweep focus solely on your passive verbs. The liability with passive verbs is that they carry absolutely no imagery. Thus, they rob the reader of his or her ability to feel, hear, see, smell, or taste in reaction to your work.

Too many passive verbs, especially in a row, will bore your reader or even possibly put him or her to sleep. Of course, you don't want to do that to yourself, let alone someone else. So, when focusing on your passive verbs, ask yourself, in each case, if there is a way you could possibly alter your sentences and/or paragraphs to rid your manuscript of so many passive verbs, and substitute action verbs in their place.

Verbs are the pulse of each one of your sentences. They direct, project forward, and are responsible for creating the most imagery, which is what makes us feel something. When they are perfectly attuned, not only will your words sing, but a substantial portion of your adjectives and adverbs will have become obsolete as well.

On sweep six, you now need to make a pass-through to pluck out any adjectives and adverbs that are no longer needed, whose presence may be redundant and, if left untouched, may lead to your project being "wordy."

Once you have completed this step, which is designed to not only fine-tune your manuscript but also to acclimate your LCM to the deepest, expressive abilities of your AW, you are free to go on to the next phase.

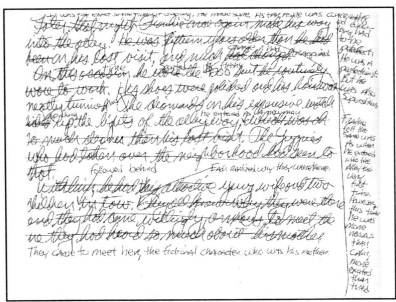

This example shows sentences rearranged,
verbs changed, and adjectives and adverbs crossed out.

The Pianist in Us All

Now it's time to type or read, if you choose to use a voice activation program, your manuscript into your computer. For this, you will need an easel or some sort of structure that will secure your large pieces of paper at eye level.

Being relaxed during this step is essential. Being relaxed ensures that you are as sensitive as possible to the flow of your material. By being as relaxed as possible, your heightened sensitivity will enable you to first sense and then smooth out any disjointed aspects of your text, which were caused by rearranging, adding, subtracting, or making general adjustments to your material.

When you have finished entering your manuscript into your computer, go on to the next step.

Let Your Computer Go to Work for You

Now is the time to let your computer go to work for you. Once your manuscript has been typed into your computer, run it through your spell check and correct any misspellings.

I am not an advocate of computerized grammar checkers. You may feel differently. If so, run your manuscript through your grammar checker as well.

Once you have run it through your spell check, and possibly through your grammar checker, print out a hardcopy of your manuscript.

One Final Read-Through

During this final phase, you may find yourself feeling ambivalent. One part of you will be wildly excited to get this project completed, while the other side of you will be feeling sad. This is normal. What you have written is like your literary child. There is a part of you that is anxious for your child to leave, while there is another portion that is terribly sad at having to say good-bye. As you read over your manuscript one last time, it is important to check for any necessary, flow-based adjustments that may need to be made.

It is also important to keep in mind that your literary child will be with you always. No matter where the two of you choose to venture from this point forward, the connection, love, and interchange that has been shared will always be a part of you.

Finish reading through your manuscript one final time and then move on to the final section.

Crossing the
Finish Line

YOUR BOOK IS NOW DONE, COMPLETED, FINISHED, AND YOUR life and the lives of so many around you, in ways you may not even be able to see, have been bettered by what you have done. Let's take a little time to reflect back so you may fully acknowledge and embrace all that has transpired.

What I Have Discovered About Myself

1. Enter into your CCM-connected state, with which you should be so familiar by now.

2. While there, focus on the words "What I have discovered."

3. Once you begin to feel, open up your eyes and write whatever it is you are feeling. Even if it takes several sessions to express whatever is coming out, don't move on until what you are feeling has been fully released.

4. Once you have completed your work with the above, do the same with each the following statements:

"*Who I really am.*"

"*Reasons I have to celebrate.*"

Your Next Book

If you heeded my words in the last chapter about beginning to release your next book, book number two is probably streaming out of you already. If it is something that you have determined you want to stay with, then do so. If not, it will be waiting around for you whenever you want to plug back into it and, by now, you certainly know how to do that.

If you choose to continue working on the writing of your second book using this system, there is plenty of good news. Because of *"the dues"* you paid in getting beyond and above all that was holding back the true you, much of what you did previously to prepare for this journey doesn't need to be done. In fact, you can skip everything that preceded the writing of your book.

A novel is a mirror walking along a main road.

Stendhal

Yes, that's correct. There's no need to focus any further on the 17 Writing Principles at the beginning of this book. You can also skip doing a contract. Just keep writing the book, and when you finish you can go straight to the revision stage. Once there, you will do your read-through, make any major structural changes that are necessary for your book, finish your post-writing research, and then go directly to typing your manuscript into your computer and performing your final read-through.

That's correct. You won't have to do any of the enhancing with the markers and different parts of speech. For if you properly completed that phase with your last book, your LCM should have already been retrained to let through and no longer inhibit the depth of your AW as it comes flying through you. Of course, this will result in a fine-tuned, deeply expressive, flowing writing style, which best depicts your voice.

If you choose to continue to author books, you now know what to do. Just follow what you did with the release of your second book and keep going, book after book after book.

If wisdom were offered me with the proviso
that I should keep it shut up and refrain from
declaring it, I should refuse. There's no delight in
owning anything unshared."

Seneca, 1at Century, A.D.

Publication and Sharing

I have to admit that I feel a significant ambivalence when speaking to you about both publishing and sharing, for in a certain way I see them as one and the same.

In one regard, I do not feel that the success of an author is determined by whether he or she has been published and/or by how many books were sold as a result. As I said, I feel that the benefits of a book run much deeper and are way more valuable than that.

However, at the same time, I almost feel as if you have a responsibility to share what the Divine released through you with others who could most benefit. As you can see, from the previous page, sharing what she wrote made all the difference for my student Debbie Blais.

So if this is an area in which you feel drawn, I suggest reading my book *You Were Born to Be. . . Published*, which lays out everything you need to know about entering the publishing world, your alternatives once there, and, in general, how to get your material in print.

In regard to the general sharing of what writing has done for you and why, because I believe everyone has a book within them, I am a strong advocate.

My suggestion to you, though, is never to offer insight or advice unless asked. The student should always seek the teacher, never vice versa.

So I suggest that you just let people know you have written a book. If your mere mentioning of that fact spikes their interest, offer them some further insights, answer their questions, recommend this book, or whatever.

Either way, as always, and especially from this point forward-to thine own, Divine self be true.

The most important thing is to be whatever
you are without shame.

Rod Steiger

Success Story by Deborah Tyler Blais

From: Deborah Tyler Blais, Florida
To: Tom Bird
Author: *Letting Your Heart Sing*

My schedule is a little fuller than I anticipated, but I love it. After the book had been out about four months, the tide turned, and I no longer had to bang on doors, send e-mails, or make phone calls to book dates for book signings or talks. Word of mouth traveled fast, and people and organizations began vying for my time! Yesterday, I met Rosie O'Donnell and gave her a book (who knows where that may lead). And a member of one of my spiritual groups was a producer with the Oprah Show for seven years. He LOVES the book and is doing everything he can to help me get the book on Oprah.

I can hardly keep up with the correspondence from readers and keep getting asked, 'When is the Workbook coming out?' I am currently working on it and expect it will be out next year. I don't know how this happened, but 'Letting Your Heart Sing' made its way into a women's prison, and they have started a Bliss Group there and are using the tools in my book to change their lives, so that when they get out, they do not have to return to a life of crime. Instead, they can live the lives they were always meant to. I can't tell you how much joy and gratitude that brings me. So, Tom, in ways you can't even imagine, the work we did together continues to transform lives everywhere.

I refer people to your web site constantly, so don't think I'm not thinking about you, I am. And I can't thank you enough for helping me fulfill my deepest heart's desire: to share my stories in such a way as to inspire others to follow their heart's desires, so that they too can experience the indescribable joy that comes from letting their heart sing.

About the Author

A Quick History of
The Tom Bird Method™

TWENTY-FOUR YEARS AGO TOM BIRD WAS A PUBLICIST WITH the Pittsburgh Pirates. However, like so many in the world, at heart he was a writer.

Tom had tried every orthodox method possible to become the successful author he felt himself to be, but nothing had worked. Not willing to believe he had been blessed with a dream, but without a way to live it, Tom developed his own system for both writing and publishing. This system is now referred to as *The Tom Bird Method*™.

Within four weeks of employing his method, Tom landed a literary agent who, at the time, was the most renowned in publishing history. Six weeks later, Tom's first book was sold to Harper & Row, then the third largest publisher in the world, for a price equivalent to three times Tom's annual salary with the Pirates. This enabled him to resign from his position and write full-time.

Shortly after Tom's first book was released, he was overwhelmed with calls from aspiring authors wondering how someone so young as he had done it. Tom responded to their queries by offering a series of classes at local Pittsburgh colleges and universities. Soon, word spread of the simple, direct. and effective methods he taught, creating nationwide demand.

Over the last quarter of a century, Tom has remained committed to sharing his method with writers all across the globe. He has made over 3000 lecture appearances before more than 50,000 students at over 110 different campuses.

Just a few of the colleges and universities which Tom has appeared at are Duke, William and Mary, Temple, Ohio State, Penn State, University of North Carolina, University of Florida, University of Arizona, University of Texas, and Emory University.

Tom has authored sixteen books and has articles in over fifty different publications.

His books are:

Willie Stargell co-authored with Willie Stargell (Harper & Row, 1984)

Tom Bird's Selective Guide to Literary Agents (Sojourn, 1985)

How to Get Published (Sojourn, 1986)

KnuckleBALLS co-authored with Phil Niekro (Freundlich Books, 1986)

Literary Law (Sojourn, 1986)

Beyond Words (Sojourn, 1987)

POWs of WWII: Forgotten Men Tell Their Stories (Praeger, 1990)

Fifty-Two Weeks or Less to the Completion of Your First Book (Sojourn, 1990)

The Author's Den, An Interactive Computer Program (Sojourn, 1993)

Hawk co-authored with Andre Dawson (Zondervan, 1994)

Hawk the Children's Version (Zondervan, 1995)

Get Published Now! (Sojourn, 2001)

The Spirit of Publishing (Sojourn, 2003)

Releasing Your Artist Within (Sojourn, 2004)

You Were Born to Be. . . Published (Sojourn, 2006)

The list of periodicals which have published Tom's work is extensive. *Parade, USA Today, Popular Mechanics,* and *The Pittsburgh Post-Gazette* are but a few of them.

Tom also hosts intensive retreats, including one on book publicity and promotion. As a publicist, Tom's career began in 1979, when he was hired by the Pittsburgh Pirates. They captured the World Series that year, affording Tom with a wealth of hands-on experience with the media.

Over his next three seasons, Tom served as the team's official spokesperson. He held press conferences, scheduled talk show appearances, supervised publicity campaigns and addressed the requests of small market media, major magazines and newspapers, and television networks.

Tom transferred his expertise in publicity to his career in publishing when his first book was released by Harper & Row in 1984. He handled the publicity tours of his next three books as well.

Over the last twenty-two years, he has utilized his publicity expertise to sell more than 98,000 copies of his self-published books.

> *Tom's charismatic personality and zest make him a natural for any type of media appearance, no matter who the audience."*
> Susan Harrow, marketing and media coach and author of "Sell Yourself Without Selling Your Soul" (Harper Resource, 2002).

As with the number of periodicals which have published work written by Tom, the number of publications which have featured articles on Tom is far-reaching. *The Los Angeles Times, Toronto Sun, Atlanta Journal-Constitution,* and *San Francisco Chronicle* have all featured articles about Tom or his work. Newspapers and periodicals in nearly all the major cities in the US have covered him, including *The Washington Post, Chicago Sun Times, Boston Globe* and *Herald, New York Times,* and *Miami Herald.*

The same goes for television and radio shows, and/or stations which have featured either Tom or his work. A handful of them include *The David Letterman Show, The Tonight Show, The Today Show, CBS Morning News,* and *The Charlie Rose Show.*

Tom was born and raised in Erie, Pennsylvania, and now lives in Sedona, Arizona with his partner, Tammy, and their daughter, Skyla. They share their home with two dogs, Rikka and Jada, five cats, and two birds.

Tom's interests include yoga, eating vegan, hiking, basketball, football, baseball, climbing, camping, racquetball, working out, playing cards and reading.

To get in touch with

Tom Bird

explore his services or find
and when he will be teaching,
either visit his website at:

www.TomBird.com

or call his office at:

928-203-0265

Printed in the United States
89153LV00003BA/295-339/A